Editor

Heather Douglas

Illustrator

Mark Mason

Cover Artist

Denise Bauer

Editor in Chief

Ina Massler Levin, M.A.

Creative Director

Karen J. Goldfluss, M.S. Ed.

Art Coordinator

Renée Christine Yates

Imaging

James Edward Grace

Publisher

Mary D. Smith, M.S. Ed.

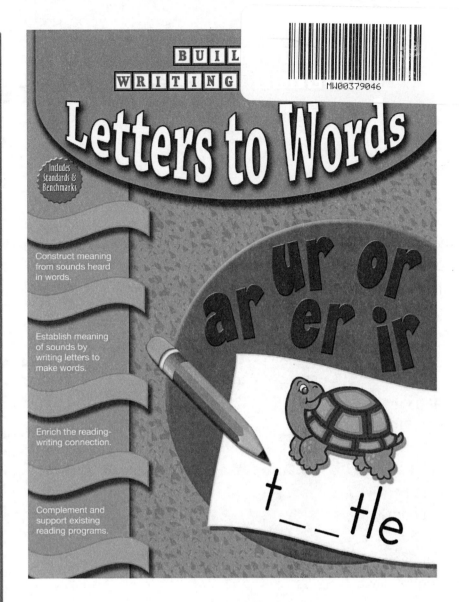

BUIL
WRITING
Letters to Words

Includes Standards & Benchmarks

Construct meaning from sounds heard in words.

Establish meaning of sounds by writing letters to make words.

Enrich the reading-writing connection.

Complement and support existing reading programs.

ar ur or er ir

t _ _ tle

Authors

Kathy Dickinson Crane M. Ed. &
Kathleen Law M. Ed.

Teacher Created Resources, Inc.

12621 Western Avenue
Garden Grove, CA 92841
www.teachercreated.com

ISBN: 978-1-4206-3246-0

©2010 Teacher Created Resources, Inc.

Reprinted, 2017

Made in U.S.A.

Teacher Created Resources

Table of Contents

Introduction 3

Writing Standards 4

The Final Frontier Sound Game 5

The Vowels – Medial Sounds. 8

Where Is the Sound?. 9

Sound Bingo 10

Dragon Land Segmenting 12

Around the Room 15

What Is The Word? 18

Writing Three-Sound Words. 19

Consonant-Vowel-Consonant Writing 20

Writing Four-Sound Words. 21

Word Families

   -at Family 22

   -og Family. 23

   -um Family 24

   -et Family 25

   -in Family 26

   -ot Family 27

   -ug Family. 28

   -ill Family 29

   -ike Family 30

   -ook Family. 31

   -ock Family. 32

   -an Family. 33

   -ump Family 34

   -ay Family. 35

   -ing Family 36

Building Words With Silent E 37

Silent E Relay 38

R-Controlled Vowels 40

Word Family. 41

Dear Friend 42

Black-Out (Sight-Word Writing) 43

Chalkboard Challenge. 46

Answer Key 48

Introduction

When writing is considered an important component of the reading process, amazing things can happen. Writing, after all, is the expression of the things learned. It is an active process when students are allowed to discover, reflect, and create. Higher-order thinking skills are awakened as students analyze, synthesize, construct meaning, and make connections through use of the written word. Research has shown that reading and writing are co-dependent and the relationship thereof is that one cannot exist to full potential without the other; both reading and write facilitate the other.

In order for students to optimize benefit from the writing process, effective writing strategies will allow students to expand the natural thinking process and transform that thinking into the written word.

Building Writing Skills—Letters to Words, if used in tandem with reputable reading and writing programs, will enable students to establish crucial skills and gain confidence in application of the alphabetic principal in regards to the representation of the written word. As students participate in the activities and worksheets within this book, they will be able to construct meaning from sounds heard within words and establish meaning of those sounds by writing letters to make words. Each activity within this book meets one or more of the McREL standards/benchmarks for the area of language arts which can be found on page 4.

Writing Standards

Each lesson in *Building Writing Skills—Letters to Words* meets one or more of the following language arts standards, which are used with permission from McREL (Copyright 2009, McREL, Mid-continent Research for Education and Learning. Telephone: 303-337-0990. Website: *www.mcrel.org*).

Standard	Pages
Uses the general skills and strategies of the writing process.	
• Uses prewriting strategies to plan written work (e.g., discusses ideas with peers, draws pictures to generate ideas, writes key thoughts and questions, rehearses ideas, records reactions and observations)	22, 28, 32
• Uses writing and other methods (e.g., using letters or phonetically spelled words, telling, dictating, making lists) to describe familiar persons, places, objects or experiences	21, 26, 37
• Writes in a variety of forms or genres (e.g., picture books, friendly letters, stories, poems, information pieces, invitations, personal experience narratives, messages, responses to literature)	29, 31, 36, 42
• Writes for different purposes (e.g., to entertain, inform, learn, communicate ideas)	23, 30, 35
Uses grammatical and mechanical conventions in written compositions.	
• Uses conventions of print in writing (e.g., forms letters in print, uses upper- and lowercase letters of the alphabet, spaces words and sentences, writes from left-to-right and top-to-bottom, includes margins	29, 40
• Uses complete sentences in written compositions	24, 34
• Uses nouns in written compositions (e.g., nouns for simple objects, family members, community workers, etc.)	41, 46–47
• Uses verbs in written compositions (e.g., verbs for a variety of situations, action words)	46–47
• Uses adjectives in written compositions (i.e., uses descriptive words)	46–47
• Uses adverbs in written compositions (i.e., uses words that answer how, when, where, and why questions)	46–47
• Uses conventions of spelling in written compositions (e.g., spells high frequency, commonly misspelled words from appropriate grade-level lists; spells phonetically regular words; uses letter-sound relationships; spells basic short vowel, long vowel, r-controlled, and consonant blend patterns; uses a dictionary and other resources to spell words)	5–7, 8, 9, 10–11, 12–14, 16–19, 20, 25, 27, 33, 38–39, 43–45

The Final Frontier Sound Game

Objective
Identifying final sounds

Preparation
Copy the space game board found on page 6 onto cardstock. Color if desired and laminate for durability.

Materials
The Final Frontier game board, Final Frontier word list (page 7), a number die, game markers, pencils, and small pieces of paper.

Directions

1. Place the game board in the center of the group and have each player put a game piece on START. Give each student a small piece of paper and a pencil.

2. Have the first player roll the die and move that many spaces.

3. Read the first word on the list. Ask the player to identify the final sound of the word.

4. Next, have the player name the letter that makes that sound. If he/she can name the matching letter, the player can move forward one more space.

5. **Note:** The letter that the student names may not be the actual spelling for a particular word. Accept either the common letter for the sound or the spelling for the sound in the word. For instance, for the word *scissors* the student should name /z/ as the final sound. Accept *z* as the common letter for the sound or *s* as the spelling for the sound in this word.

6. Finally, have all players write the identified letter on paper.

7. If the student cannot name the final sound of the word, repeat the word and slightly emphasize the sound.

8. The player must then move back one space. Tell the student the letter for the final sound and have him/her write it on the page as a practice and review activity.

9. Proceed to the next player and repeat the process.

10. Continue around the group. To keep everyone engaged throughout the game, have all players write the letter each time a final sound is identified.

11. If time permits, play the game again after a student arrives at FINISH.

The Final Frontier Game Mat

The Final Frontier Word List

Sun	/n/	Explore	/r/	Flag	/g/
Star	/r/	Scientist	/t/	Scissors	/z/
Planet	/t/	Alien	/n/	Gym	/m/
Earth	/th/	Crew	/oo/	Library	/e/
Comet	/t/	Captain	/n/	Number	/r/
Space	/s/	Command	/d/	Letters	/z/
Mars	/z/	Doctor	/r/	Boy	/oy/
Venus	/s/	Nurse	/s/	Girl	/l/
Mercury	/e/	Hospital	/l/	Man	/n/
Jupiter	/r/	Sick	/k/	Woman	/n/
Saturn	/n/	Bay	/a/	Office	/s/
Pluto	/o/	Transport	/t/	Principal	/l/
Uranus	/s/	Food	/d/	Computer	/r/
Neptune	/n/	Chair	/r/	Desk	/k/
Asteroid	/d/	Table	/l/	Glue	/oo/
Meteor	/r/	Couch	/ch/	Marker	/r/
Rocket	/t/	Stove	/v/	Crayon	/n/
Spaceship	/p/	Door	/r/	Cubby	/e/
Orbit	/t/	Lamp	/p/	Pencil	/l/
Capsule	/l/	Bed	/d/	Red	/d/
Astronaut	/t/	Cabin	/n/	Blue	/oo/
Satellite	/t/	Furniture	/r/	Black	/k/
Launch	/ch/	School	/l/	Green	/n/
Lift-off	/f/	Teacher	/r/	Orange	/j/
Observe	/v/	Bus	/s/	Jump	/p/

Name _____

The Vowels—Medial Sounds

 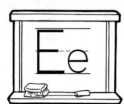 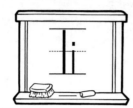 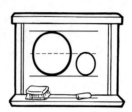 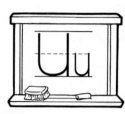

Directions

Each picture below contains a medial vowel sound. Say the name of the picture and write the missing vowel sound in the middle of each word.

f___g	h___t	b___g
m___n	n___t	t___n
c___p	s___n	w___b

Name: _____

Where Is the Sound?

Directions

Say the name of each picture. Circle the first letter if you hear its sound at the beginning of the word. Circle the middle letter if you hear its sound in the middle of the word. Circle the last letter if you hear its sound at the end of the word.

s s s	c c c	e e e
u u u	n n n	m m m
a a a	a a a	s s s
o o o	t t t	e e e
b b b	i i i	l l l

Sound Bingo

Objective
Identifying sounds in words

Preparation
Copy the Sound Bingo Cards found on page 11 on cardstock. Laminate for durability. Cut the cards apart.

Materials
Sound Bingo cards, word list, bingo markers.

Directions
2–6 Players

1. Give each player a Sound Bingo card. Place the bingo markers within easy reach.

2. Read a word from the word list at the bottom of the page.

3. Ask one player to identify the initial sound of the word. Direct all the students to check for that sound's letter on their cards. Students with that letter should cover it with a bingo marker.

4. Repeat the word and have another player identify the medial sound. Direct students to check the middle column for that sound's letter and cover it with a bingo marker if found.

5. Say the word again and have a third player identify the final sound. Tell all the students to look for that sound's letter in the third column, covering the letter if it is there.

6. Read another word from the list and repeat the steps. As the students are able, combine steps in order to increase the pace of the game.

7. Continue playing until a student calls out BINGO, indicating that he/she has every space on the card covered.

8. Exchange cards and begin again. Add additional words to the list, including long vowel words, if desired.

Sound Bingo Word List

bell	cake	hill	wag	bed	queen	rug	cat
toss	fox	nap	vet	tom	fun	right	jig
buzz	yak	vine	web	job	hum	quiz	yes
cup	nod	fix	hop	rock	tub	jam	wax

Sound Bingo (cont.)

Sound Bingo

Initial	Medial	Final
b	e	z
Initial	Medial	Final
h	u	l
Initial	Medial	Final
q	i	s

Sound Bingo

Initial	Medial	Final
s	i	d
Initial	Medial	Final
j	a	n
Initial	Medial	Final
y	o	x

Sound Bingo

Initial	Medial	Final
v	a	g
Initial	Medial	Final
l	i	r
Initial	Medial	Final
w	u	k

Sound Bingo

Initial	Medial	Final
c	o	f
Initial	Medial	Final
t	e	p
Initial	Medial	Final
n	a	m

Dragon Land

Objective

Reinforcing student's ability to synthesize words from their separate phonemes.

Materials

Picture cards of two- and three-sound words in a box or bag, a dragon playing card and a small container of bingo chips for each student.

Preparation

Seat the students at a table and give each a dragon playing card that has been copied from page 14 and a small container containing three bingo chips. Copy and laminate picture cards found on page 13 and put them in a box (or bag). During the play, the teacher will draw and discard all cards thus allowing students to be free to manipulate chips.

Directions

1. Inform students they will practice blending and segmenting words while feeding dragons. Tell students the following story:

   Far away in the land of dragons there was a freakish storm. The storm was verrryyy weird and greatly affected the monstrous dragons of the land! The dragons became very hungry and they desperately craved to eat words. The first dragon to eat after the storm gobbled an entire word all at once and became very sick. The second dragon, thinking the first to be very piggish in his eating habits, ate his word one sound at a time. This tasted very delicious to the dragon. And, from that day on, the dragons in the land have eaten words only one sound at a time.

   However, there has been a great drought and *Dragon Land* has run out of food! You must help the dragons! They are starving! You have a great job to do, feed the starving dragons!

2. To begin, the teacher draws a card out of the box and tells students the name of the picture saying the word sound by sound. Each player in turn will guess the picture that is on the card. *For example if the teacher draws a card with a picture of a cat, he/she says, /c/ /a/ /t/. He/she then points to a player and asks, "do you know what is on my picture?" If that player guesses the word, he/she is asked to say the word sound by sound, isolating each sound (not letter) one by one. The teacher then places the card into a discard pile atop the mystery box.*

3. Next, the player states the word sounds while feeding his/her dragon. *The player repeats the word sound by sound as chips are placed in the appropriate circles on the dragon (first sound, first circle, etc).*

4. On each turn as the third and final chip is placed, all players say *YUM!* Then the player removes chips and places them back into his/her container.

Dragon Land *(cont.)*

sub	**gum**	**ham**
dig	**sun**	**pit**
hug	**fish**	**bag**
hot	**run**	**mug**
fat	**sit**	**web**
knot	**ship**	**top**

Dragon Land (cont.)

14

Around the Room

Objective
Blending sounds and segmenting words orally.

Preparation
Copy the Around the Room game board found on page 16 onto cardstock. Color if desired and laminate for durability.

Materials
Around the Room game board, Around the Room word list (page 17), game markers, and a die.

Directions

1. Place the game board in the center of the group and have each player put a game marker on START.

2. Players blend and segment words as they move around the room to the teacher's desk.

3. Have Player A roll the die and move that many spaces.

4. Using the word list, say the sounds for a word for Player A to blend together. For example, if the word on the list is cat, say the sounds /c/ /a/ /t/. Player A must say *cat* in order to leave his/her marker where it is. If Player A cannot put the sounds together to say the word *cat*, his/her game marker must be moved back one space.

5. Have all students segment Player A's word together before continuing the game. For the word cat, have the students say /c/ /a/ /t/ together.

6. Next, have Player B roll the die and move that many spaces. Say the sounds for him/her to blend back into a word. If the word is correct, have the students segment together. If the word is incorrect, Player B moves his/her marker back one space before everyone segments the word together.

7. Continue playing until all players reach the teacher's desk.

8. If time permits, play the game again.

Around the Room (cont.)

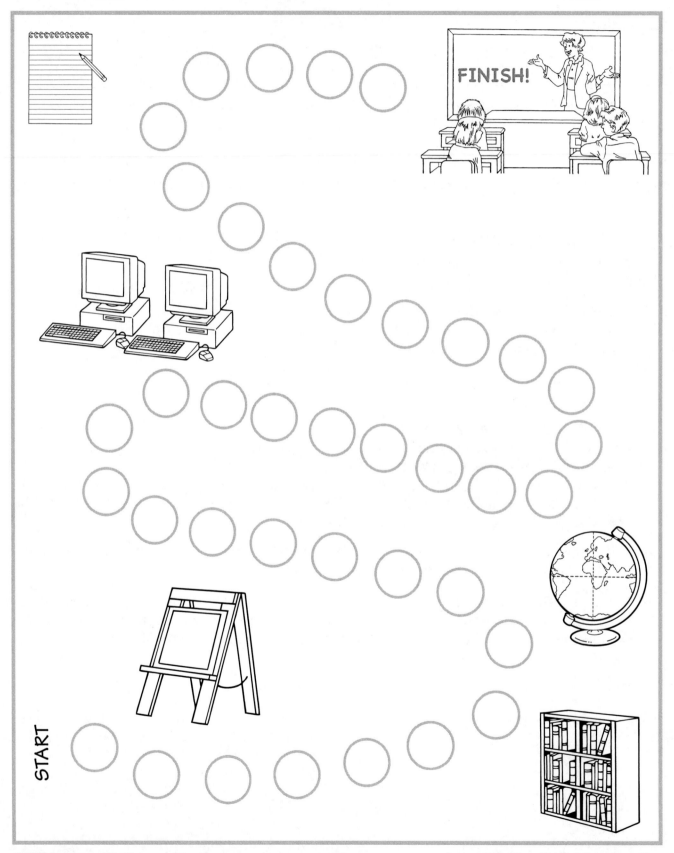

16

Around the Room (cont.)

Sounds	Word	Sounds	Word
/i/ /s/	ice	/t/ /o/ /p/	top
/b/ /e/	bee	/b/ /o/ /n/	bone
/k/ /e/	key	/k/ /a/ /n/	can
/p/ /i/	pie	/l/ /a/ /m/ /p/	lamp
/e/ /g/	egg	/t/ /r/ /u/ /k/	truck
/t/ /i/	tie	/m/ /a/ /s/ /k/	mask
/f/ /a/ /n/	fan	/s/ /k/ /a/ /t/	skate
/p/ /i/ /g/	pig	/t/ /e/ /n/ /t/	tent
/r/ /a/ /t/	rat	/s/ /n/ /a/ /k/	snack
/d/ /o/ /g/	dog	/b/ /o/ /t/ /l/	bottle
/b/ /e/ /l/	bell	/p/ /l/ /a/ /n/	plane
/h/ /o/ /z/	hose	/s/ /t/ /a/ /m/ /p/	stamp
/t/ /u/ /b/	tub	/z/ /e/ /b/ /r/ /u/	zebra
/f/ /o/ /n/	phone	/k/ /a/ /n/ /d/ /e/	candy
/m/ /o/ /p/	mop	/p/ /l/ /a/ /n/ /t/	plant
/p/ /a/ /n/	pan	/p/ /e/ /n/ /u/ /t/	peanut
/t/ /r/ /e/	tree	/r/ /o/ /b/ /o/ /t/	robot
/k/ /u/ /b/	cub	/s/ /t/ /u/ /m/ /p/	stump
/s/ /o/ /k/	sock	/s/ /p/ /i/ /d/ /r/	spider

What is the Word?

Directions

Say the name of each picture slowly to yourself listening carefully to each sound. Now write the beginning, middle, and ending sound of each word in the spaces provided.

_____ _____ _____	_____ _____ _____	_____ _____ _____
_____ _____ _____	_____ _____ _____	_____ _____ _____
_____ _____ _____	_____ _____ _____	_____ _____ _____

Name: _____

Writing Three-Sound Words

Directions

Say the name of each picture slowly to yourself listening carefully to each sound. Now write the beginning, middle, and ending sound of each word in the spaces provided.

___ ___ ___	___ ___ ___	___ ___ ___
___ ___ ___	___ ___ ___	___ ___ ___
___ ___ ___	___ ___ ___	___ ___ ___

Name: _____

Consonant-Vowel-Consonant Writing

Directions

Say the name of each picture. Listen for the initial, medial, and final sounds. Write the letters for the sounds in spaces.

Writing Four–Sound Words

Directions

Say the name of each picture. Listen for the three or four sounds in the word. Write the letters for the sounds on the lines.

Name: _____

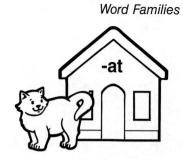

–at Family

Directions

Write six words in the box below that belong to the –at word family. Then write a story using as many of the words as possible in the box below.

-og Family

Directions

Name each picture. Complete each word by writing the initial consonant or consonant blend.

_____ og	_____ og	_____ og
_____ og	_____ og	_____ og

Directions

Use three –og family words to tell a story. Use pictures, letters, and words to record your story in this space.

–um Family

Directions

This is a little girl who loves to chew gum! She ran out and needs your help to reach the gumball machine at her favorite store. Use the letter combinations below to add a beginning sound to each –um to make a new word. When you have completed the list, draw a picture of the girl's favorite machine filled with delicious gumballs.

h	
s	
ch	
dr	
pl	
y	

_____um
_____um
_____um
_____um
_____um
_____um

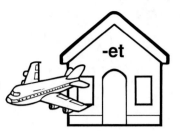

–et Family

Directions

Use the words from the –et word family to complete each sentence. Write a word from the list on the blank. Use each word one time only.

1. She hit the ball over the _____.

2. I am going to fly in a _____.

3. If you play in the rain, you will get _____.

4. I know a boy named _____.

5. I need to _____ a haircut.

6. If your dog is sick, take it to the _____.

7. The baby started to cry and _____.

8. Will your mom _____ you go?

9. Please _____ the plates on the table.

10. I _____ her at the mall.

11. He has a _____ parrot.

12. Are you done, _____ ?

get

jet

let

met

net

pet

set

vet

wet

yet

fret

Bret

–in Family

Directions

Lin has a great big grin because he can write words that belong to the *–in* word family. Can you? Use the letter combinations provided below to complete each word.

p	ch
sh	sp
tw	f
w	b

___ ___ i n

___ ___ i n

___ ___ i n

___ ___ i n

___ i n

___ i n

___ i n

___ i n

–ot Family

Directions

Make a list of *–ot* words. Beginning with the word pot, change the initial consonant *p* to the letter *c*. What is the new word? Keep changing the initial consonant to make new words in the rest of the boxes. Use the following consonants for your exchanges: d, g, h, j, l, n, r, t.

pot	
cot	

Directions

Draw a scene using one or more of the *–ot* words. Use words and sounds that you know to write about your picture.

Name: _____

-ug Family

Directions

Can you write the words that belong to the *-ug* word family? Write as many words as you can and then draw a bug of your own design in the space below.

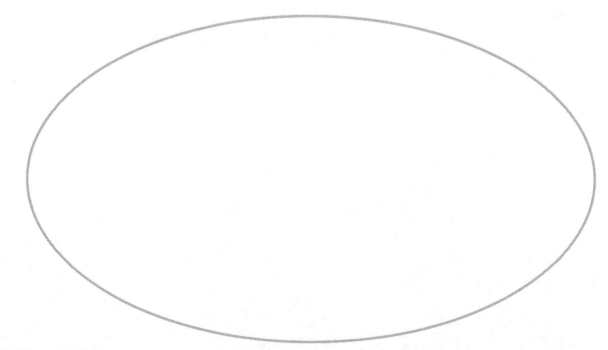

Name: _____

–ill Family

Directions

Tell a story about a boy named Bill or a girl named Jill, using four or more words from the list below.

drill	**grill**	**thrill**	**frill**	**quill**	**still**
Bill	**Jill**	**gill**	**dill**	**krill**	**trill**
fill	**sill**	**hill**	**will**	**mill**	**pill**

Directions

Draw a picture to illustrate your story. Write the –ill words from your story. Try to write other words in your story, too. Stretch out words by saying them slowly, listening for individual sounds. Write down the letters that match the sounds that you hear.

Name: _____

-ike

–ike Family

Directions

Read (or have someone read) the following story. Underline every word that belongs in the –ike word family.

Mike and Spike

I know a boy named Mike. He has a dog called Spike. Mike and Spike like to have fun together.

Yesterday, Mike rode his bike to a baseball game. After getting one strike, Mike hit the ball onto the field. Before anyone could reach the ball, Spike caught it in his mouth and ran away with it! When the game ended, Mike got on his bike. Spike wanted a ride. He jumped on a trike and tried to follow Mike!

Tomorrow Mike's family is taking a trip to the mountains. Mike wants to hike up to the pike of the tallest mountain. What do you think Spike will do?

Directions

Draw a picture of Mike and Spike. Write Mike's and Spike's names by their picture. Label other pictures by saying the words slowly and writing the sounds that you hear.

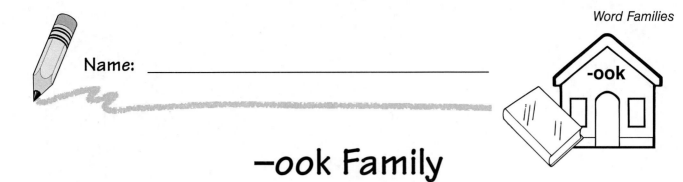

–ook Family

Directions

Use the –ook family words in the box to complete the poem. Choose the word that best completes each line of the poem and write it on the line.

hook	book	Brook	nook	cook

There once was a girl named _____.

She caught a fish on a _____.

As she waited for it to _____,

she read a _____

in a _____.

Directions
Draw a picture to illustrate the poem.

–ock Family

Directions

Write six words that belong to the *–ock* family in the spaces below.

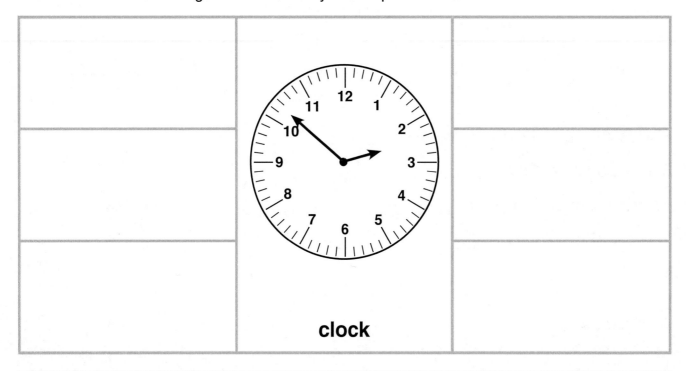

clock

Directions

Draw a picture to go along with one or more of the -ock words. Write about your picture, using words and sounds that you know.

–an Family

Directions

Look at the picture scene below and circle all of the pictures that end in the sound –*an*. Then in the space below, write the words.

Challenge: Can you write 3 more –*an* word family words?

–ump Family

Directions

Read the sentence and the three *–ump* family words under the sentence. Choose the word that best completes the sentence and write it on the line.

1. Did you _____ your head on the door?

      bump   lump   jump

2. Did the camel have one _____ or two?

      gump   lump   hump

3. I need to use a _____ to put air in the tire.

      trump   pump   dump

4. How many times can you _____ ?

      chump   slump   jump

5. The truck will take our trash to the _____ .

      dump   pump   clump

6. He is sitting on the _____ of an old tree.

      trump   stump   plump

7. I found a _____ in my mashed potatoes.

      crump   lump   gump

8. My cat is not fat, just a little _____ !

      plump   chump   bump

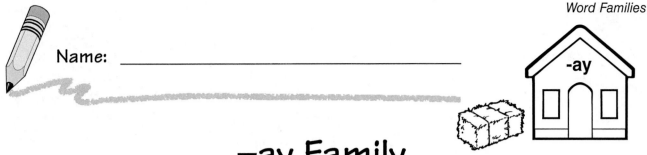

Name: _____

−ay Family

Directions
Read (or have someone read) the following story. Underline every word that belongs in the *−ay* word family.

Zay and Jay

Zay and Jay are best friends. Their moms say they just like to play. Zay's mom gave the boys some clay. They made zoo animals to lay on a tray. Jay's mom said she would pay for a trip to the zoo the next day.

On another day, Zay and Jay went to play with their friend Kay. They had fun playing in a field of hay until the last ray of sun faded.

In May, Zay and Jay spent the day at the bay. They had fun playing in the water. They wanted to stay even when the day turned gray!

Directions
What else could Zay and Jay do? Draw a picture of Jay and Zay having a great day! Label or write Zay's and Jay's names by their pictures. Label any other pictures by saying the words slowly and writing sounds that you hear.

–ing Family

Directions

Tell a story about a king, using four or more words from the list below.

bing	ding	sling	swing	string
wing	zing	fling	cling	bling
ring	sing	ping	sting	bring

Directions

Draw a picture to illustrate your story. Write the –ing words from your story. Try to write other words in your story, too. Stretch out words by saying them slowly, listening for individual sounds. Write down letters that match the sounds you hear.

Name: _____

Building Words Using the Silent E

Directions

Change the words below into new words by adding a silent e to the end of each. Write a story below using some of these new words.

cap ____	mad ____	scrap ____
rag ____	spin ____	bit ____
rid ____	pin ____	con ____
hop ____	hug ____	slim ____

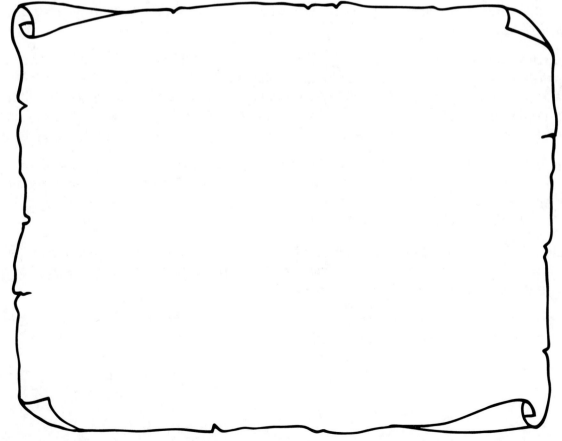

Silent E Relay

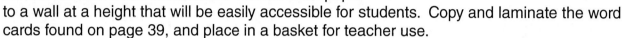

Objective
Developing confidence using the silent e to change vowel sounds within words, making new words.

Preparation
Using two large sheets of butcher paper, create two lists of ten identical words using the list below. Write the words in large block letters neatly printed using a list format. Laminate each sheet. Fasten each paper to a wall at a height that will be easily accessible for students. Copy and laminate the word cards found on page 39, and place in a basket for teacher use.

Word List: dim, pin, con, tap, pal, man, ton, can, mad, hop (*additional words that may be used for variety:* cut, cod, fat, nod, kit, mat, pan)

Materials
Butcher paper lists, a dry erase marker and eraser for each team member, teacher calling cards in a basket, a discard box, and a timer.

Directions
1. Divide students into two teams and queue each behind a starting line. The teacher will be the caller and stand near the two lists affixed to the wall with the basket of word cards and discard box.

2. **Instruct teams to do the following:** When the teacher draws out and calls a word, the first team member must look carefully at the list and run forward to add or subtract an *e* to make that word appear on the list. For example, if the teacher calls "dime," the first player from each team will run forward and add an *e* to the end of *dim* using his/her dry erase marker. When finished, those team members will run to the back of their respective lines.

3. The teacher will then call another word. *If this new word has previously had a silent e added, the students run forward to erase the e from the list to change it into the word called. (For example, if the word called is dim and an e had been previously added changing the word to dime, the e must be erased to make the new word).*

4. Students must be reminded to think carefully to decide each turn if their word will require a marker, an eraser, or if the word is correct as is. ***Note:*** *Instruct students to simply run to the word and tap it lightly if it is correct.*

5. To add competition to the game, set a timer for 5 minutes and see if the teams can make all word changes within the allotted time.

Silent E Relay *(cont.)*

dim	pin	con	tap
pal	man	ton	can
mad	hop	dime	pine
cone	tape	pale	mane
tone	cane	made	hope
sit	rid	cub	bit
cap	rip	van	rat
wag	fin	site	ride
cube	bite	cape	ripe
vane	rate	wage	fine

R-Controlled Vowels

Directions

The following words have a vowel followed by an *r*. Complete the spelling of each word by adding an r-controlled vowel. Using one of the following for each word: *-ar, -er, -ir, -ur, -or*

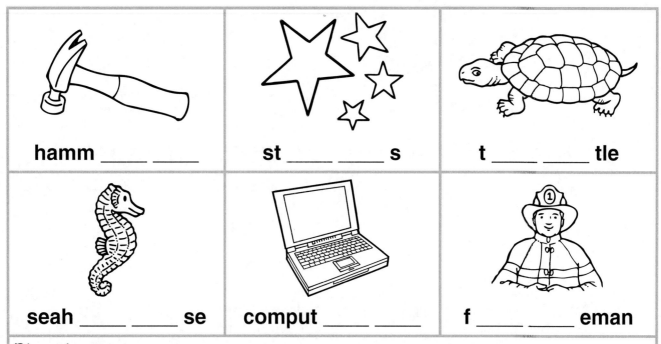

hamm ____ ____

st ____ ____ s

t ____ ____ tle

seah ____ ____ se

comput ____ ____

f ____ ____ eman

Directions

Draw a scene using one or more of the r-controlled vowel pictures in your illustration. Use words and sounds that you know to write about your scene.

Word Families

Directions

Look at the scene below and circle pictures that belong to the word families listed above. Write each word in the box below.

Name: _____

Dear Friend

Directions

Use some of the words below to write a letter to a friend.

star	cake	hat
jig	like	sing
hug	get	book

○   Dear Friend,

_____

_____

_____

_____

_____

_____

_____

_____

○ _____

_____

_____

_____

From, _____

_____

Black-Out

Objective
Writing sight words fluently.

Materials
A poster with sight words clearly displayed, a pencil, a set of sight word flash cards, highlighter and worksheet for each player, 1-minute, 2-minute, and 3-minute timers.

Preparation:
Copy the sight word cards found on page 44, laminate and cut. Note: Make more flash cards and posters as needed to personalize the game for spelling units, etc.

Directions

1. Pass a pencil and a worksheet to each student. Display the poster in clear view of the students.

2. Show the students the timer and explain that the timer will allow students to write as many words as they can in (1, 2, or 3) minutes. *Vary the time according to the ability of the groups. Use the shortest time possible to complete the task to increase fluency.*

3. **Note:** The teacher reminds students they will need to write quickly, but must write the words neatly as they will need to be easily read.

4. After instructions are clearly given to the students, the teacher turns on the 3-minute timer and says GO. Students then write the sight words randomly, one in each square on their worksheets. *If students struggle, the teacher should offer as much assistance as necessary. At the end of the allotted time, the teacher calls STOP.*

5. Place the sight word pile in front of the teacher, collect pencils and give each student a highlighter.

6. Tell students that a sight word will be drawn from a pile one at a time and read by the teacher. Students will then be detectives and find that word on their worksheets, circling the word with a highlighter. *After the word is stated, pause, and then show the sight word card for additional support.*

7. The pace of reading and detecting the sight words should move quickly. Instruct students to yell "BLACK-OUT!" when all words are detected on their sheets.

Black Out (cont.)

and	big	can
come	down	for
little	look	like
now	give	put
has	was	ask
after	good	how
just	over	are

Black-Out *(cont.)*

45

Chalkboard Challenge

Objective
Using sounds to write nouns, verbs, adjectives, and adverbs.

Preparation
Copy the Chalkboard Challenge Word List found on page 47.

Materials
Chalkboard Challenge Word List (page 47), chalk, erasers, one or more chalkboards—players may share one large chalkboard or they may each have a small individual chalkboard to use.

Directions
1. During this game you will refer to each set of words as nouns, verbs, adjectives, or adverbs. The students do not need to identify them as such or define these terms. The lists are categorized in this way to help introduce these parts of speech to the students.

2. Divide the players into two teams and direct one player from each team to go to the board to write out the sounds of a word.

3. Read a word from the noun word list. Identify it as a noun and direct the first two players to write the sounds for the word on the board.

4. Check the spelling of the word for each player. Give teams one point for every sound of the word that is written. For instance, if the word is *nest* and the player writes NST, his/her team earns three points. Although the emphasis is on writing letters to match sounds, if a student is able to correctly spell a word (writing *plane* instead of *plan*), award one extra point.

5. Record the score and have the next two players go to the board. Read the next noun and have the students write the sounds they hear. Count the number of correct sounds written and record the points.

6. After all players spell a noun, change to the verb list. Identify the words as verbs and say the first word for the first two players to spell. After all players spell a verb, change to the adjective list, and then to the adverb list.

7. Continue playing, going back through the various word lists. Identify the type of word that the students will spell with each change.

8. The first team to reach 50 points wins the game. If time permits, mix up the teams and begin again.

9. Adapt this game to meet the needs of the players. Increase or decrease the number of points needed to win. Add simpler or more difficult words to the list if needed.

Chalkboard Challenge *(cont.)*

Nouns

mom	disk
dad	tent
cat	bottle
dog	clock
tub	slide
pig	mask
fan	zebra
mop	stump
nest	spider
plane	robot

Verbs

run	taste
pack	touch
play	smell
ride	drive
fly	jump
roll	sing
read	swim
sit	dance
paint	crawl
skate	stamp

Adjectives

red	cold
big	black
hot	funny
bad	clean
old	ugly
dull	lazy
light	pretty
cute	fancy
little	sleepy
soft	crazy

Adverbs

more	shyly
less	madly
soon	kindly
not	likely
fast	badly
last	slowly
even	quickly
oddly	easily
only	quietly
fully	softly

Answer Key

Page 8

Write the letters: i, a, u, a, e, e, a, u, e

Page 9

Circle the letter in the appropriate placement; initial, initial, medial, medial, final, initial, initial, medial, final, medial, final, final, initial, medial, final

Page 10

b-e-l, k-a-k, h-i-l, w-a-g, b-e-d, kw-e-n, r-u-g, k-a-t, t-o-s, f-o-ks, n-a-p, v-e-t, t-o-m, f-u-n. r-i-t, j-i-g, b-u-z, y-a-k, v-i-n, w-e-bm j-o-b, h-u-m, kw-i-z, y-e-s, k-u-p, n-o-d, f-i-ks, h-o-p, r-o-k, t-u-b, j-a-m. w-a-ks

Page 13

s-u-b, g-u-m. h-a-m, d-i-g, s-u-n, p-i-t, h-u-g, f-i-s-h, n-a-g, h-o-t, r-u-n, m-u-g, f-a-t, s-i-t, r-i-g, n-o-t, sh-i-p, t-o-p

Page 18

sub, gum, lid, zip, pot, cat, dog, fan, pig

Page 19

hop, dig, wig, rat, hat, bat, net, rug, bug

Page 20

dog, cup, pin, sun, tub, cap, map, mop, van, log, jet, bib

Page 21

mask, tent, nest, milk, flag, frog, stop, swim, vest

Page 24

hum, sum, chum, drum, plum, yum (in any order)

Page 25

1. net
2. jet
3. wet
4. Bret
5. get
6. vet
7. fret
8. let
9. set
10. met
11. pet
12. yet

Page 26

shin, chin, twin, spin, bin, pin, win, fin

Page 27

dot, got, hot, jot, lot, not, rot, tot (in any order)

Page 30

Mike, Spike, Mike, Spike, Mike, Spike, like, Mike, bike, strike, Mike, Spike, Mike, Bike, Spike, trike, Mike, Mike's, Mike, hike, pike, Spike

Page 31

Brook, hook, cook, book, nook

Page 33

can, fan, man, pan, van, ran

Page 34

1. bump
2. hump
3. pump
4. jump
5. dump
6. stump
7. lump
8. plump

Page 35

Zay, Jay, Zay, Jay, say, play, Zay's, clay, lay, tray, Jay's, pay, day, day, Zay, Jay, play, Kay, (playing), hay, ray, May, Zay, Jay, day, bay, (playing), stay, day, gray

Page 40

hammer, stars, turtle, seahorse, computer, fireman

Page 41

net, cup, man, fin, jet, van, pup, pin